H IS FOR HAWKEYE

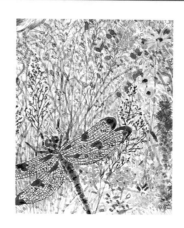

Jay Wagner

Illustrated by
Eileen Potts Dawson

TRAILS BOOKS
Black Earth, Wisconsin

Library of Congress Control Number: 2003105890
ISBN: 1-931599-11-4

Editor: Stan Stoga
Designer: Kortney Kaiser

Printed in China by Four Colour Imports.

07 06 05 04 03   6 5 4 3 2 1

Trails Books, a division of Trails Media Group, Inc.
P.O. Box 317 • Black Earth, WI 53515
(800) 236-8088 • e-mail: books@wistrails.com
www.trailsbooks.com

To CeCe, who gave me Zoey and Kiernan,
my two favorite little Iowans—J. W.

For D, "the keystone of my angle of repose"—E.

A is for Amana Colonies.

In the 1840s, a group of people came to this country from Germany. The group was called the Community of True Inspiration. They wanted a place to worship God without being afraid. By 1865, the group changed its name to the Amana Society. They built seven small towns on a huge piece of land near Cedar Rapids. There, the members shared chores, ate as a group, and worshipped together. They built churches, schools, bakeries, farms, and factories. The group split up in 1936. Today, the Amana Colonies are a popular tourist attraction. There, visitors can learn about the group's history.

B is for bridges.

Iowa has about a dozen covered bridges, most of which were built in the 1800s. They were covered to prevent rain and snow from damaging the wood floor. They also were a safe place for travelers caught in a storm. The state's most famous covered bridges are in Madison County, near Winterset. In the early 1990s, they were featured in a best-selling book, *The Bridges of Madison County*, which was later made into a popular movie. As a result, people come from all over the world to view the bridges.

CARTER '76

C is for caucus.

Every four years, thousands of people in Iowa meet in homes, churches, and other public places to hold political meetings called caucuses. At the gatherings, people who belong to the Democratic or Republican political parties decide on whom they want to run for president of the United States. Political meetings like these are held in other states, but Iowa's is always the first. In 1972, few people had heard of Georgia Governor Jimmy Carter. But he spent months in Iowa, meeting people and telling them why he would be a good leader. He got the most votes in these caucuses. This was a surprising victory that helped him win over voters in other states. He was elected president soon after that.

Clinton

D is for Des Moines.

Des Moines is the capital of Iowa and the largest city in the state. But when it first became the capital in 1857, only a few people were living in the area. Most of them were part of Fort Des Moines, a fur-trading post on the banks of the Des Moines and Raccoon Rivers. This settlement was very close to the center of the state. Today, Des Moines is a busy city with about 200,000 residents. Its largest businesses include insurance companies, magazine publishers, and hospitals.

E is for effigy mounds.

Almost 3,000 years ago, Native Americans began building special mounds of earth throughout the Great Lakes region. Some people think that the mounds were burial sites or places for special ceremonies. However, no one knows exactly what they were for. The mounds are built in various shapes, including animals such as eagles, falcons, bison, deer, turtles, lizards, and bears. Iowa's Effigy Mounds National Monument, along the Mississippi River near Marquette, has nearly 200 mounds. Some of them are shaped like birds and bears.

Farmington Fonda

Fairfield Farley Farmington Fayette Fonda Fontanelle Forest City Fort Dodge Fort Madison

Fairbank Fairfield Fairfax Farley Farmington Fayette Fontanelle

F is for farming.

Iowa is one of the most important food-producing areas of the world, with more than 93,000 farms within the state. One farm can grow enough food to feed about 279 people for a year. Nearly one-quarter of that amount is shipped to hungry people around the world. No other state in the nation produces more corn or pigs. Iowa also ranks second in the production of soybeans. The state is also famous for providing cattle, eggs, and milk to the rest of the world.

Fontanelle Farley

Fort Madison Fairfax

G is for glaciers.

Millions of years ago, glaciers, huge sheets of ice several miles wide, cut through the area now known as Iowa. Glaciers are known as nature's bulldozer. They leveled the earth in some places and cut deep grooves into the ground in others. As the glaciers melted, rocks and soil that were ground up under the ice were left behind. This material is called glacial till. Today, Iowa has rich, fertile farmland because of the glaciers.

Hamburg Hampton Harlan Hartley Hawarden Hedrick Hiawatha Hinton Holstein Hospers

Hedrick Hiawatha Hinton Holstein Hospers

H is for Hawkeye.

Iowa's nickname is the Hawkeye State. Many people believe this nickname honors the Indian leader Chief Black Hawk. In 1832, he led a group of Sauk and Fox Indians to try to take back land that the U.S. government had seized from his people. It did not work. Six years later, Black Hawk surrendered the last of his people's claim to Iowa lands. He said sadly: "I loved my towns, my cornfields, and the home of my people. I fought for it. It is now yours. Keep it as we did. It will produce you good crops."

I is for ice cream.

Le Mars, home of the Wells Blue Bunny ice cream plant, makes more ice cream than any other city in the world. The Wells family has been making ice cream and other frozen products here since 1925. They are sold in all 50 states and 20 foreign countries. A visitor center in Le Mars has displays on how everyone's favorite food is made. Also there is an old-fashioned ice cream parlor where people can sample their favorite flavor. Strawberry anyone?

J is for James Jordan.

James Jordan was one of a small group of brave Iowans who helped runaway slaves escape to Canada before and during the Civil War. His house in West Des Moines, now open to the public, was part of the Underground Railroad. This was a chain of hiding places where slaves spent the night resting during their long journey to freedom. There are other Iowa stops on the Underground Railroad that you can visit today. They include the Lewelling Quaker Shrine in Salem, the Hitchcock House in Lewis, and the Todd House in Tabor.

K is for Kinnick.

Nile Kinnick was one of the greatest football players in the history of the University of Iowa, but he was much more than that. In 1939, he won the Heisman Trophy, awarded to the nation's best college player. He was also a top student. Instead of playing professional football after college, he went to law school. Then, in 1941, before America entered World War II, Kinnick joined the navy. Two years later, the plane he was flying crashed and he was killed. He was 24 years old. In 1972, the university named its football stadium in honor of Kinnick.

HEISMAN

L is for Loess Hills.

The Loess Hills area is in the far western part of Iowa. It is one of only two places in the world where wind-blown soil, created by glaciers, made small mountains. Between 10,000 and 20,000 years ago, the fine soil left behind by melting glaciers was picked up by easterly winds and dropped in an area stretching 200 miles along the Missouri River. This fine soil, called loess (rhymes with "bus"), rises as high as 200 feet in some places here. This created an area with lots of different trees and plants.

M is for Music Man.

Meredith Willson based his Broadway musical The *The Music Man* on his childhood in Mason City. The play went on to become one of the most popular stage shows of all time. It was even made into a Hollywood movie. Both have been seen by many people around the world. The Music Man Square in Mason City is a modern structure built in honor of Willson. It features a street scene just like the one in the movie. Mason City is nicknamed River City because it was the model for the town in the musical.

Mason City

N is for Newton.

In 1907, Fredrick Maytag began making the world's first motor-powered washing machines in the town of Newton. Before this, people would wash their clothes by hand. The new machines became very popular. Soon, so many other companies set up plants in Newton that it earned the nickname of Washing Machine Capital of the World. Today, the Maytag Company in Newton is the second-largest appliance maker in the United States. The Maytag Lonely Repairman, seen in many commercials, is one of the most well-known characters in advertising.

O is for orphan trains.

From the mid-1850s to the 1920s, thousands of homeless children in New York City and other eastern cities were put on trains to the Midwest. They were hoping to be adopted by new families. During this time, these orphan trains carried almost 8,000 children to Iowa. Many of the orphans found good homes, but some did not. Several people did not like the idea of sending young people to live with families they did not know. As a result, the trains stopped bringing the children to the Midwest.

P is for prairie.

Before the first settlers arrived in Iowa and began to plant corn and other crops, the land was covered with tallgrass prairie. The grass in some places was over six feet high. Large areas were covered with colorful, fragrant wildflowers. Buffalo, wild turkeys, and eagles were everywhere. When the settlers arrived, much of the prairie was destroyed so that the land could be farmed. Today, some land is being restored to what it was like before the settlers.

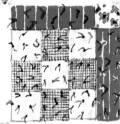

Q is for quilts.

Quilts are valuable to many Iowa families. These bed covers are often handed down from one generation to the next. Most are sewn together from small scraps of cloth. They are usually decorated with images that tell a story or have special meaning. Early pioneers on their way west used quilts in many ways. They protected travelers from cold winds and dust storms. They were used to wrap the bodies of loved ones for burial. At the end of the long trip, quilts were used to bring comfort and beauty to the pioneer's new homes.

R is for rivers.

Iowa is bordered by two of the world's greatest rivers, the Mississippi to the east and the Missouri to the west. For over two hundred years, both have been used for travel and to carry goods from one place to the next. Today, barges (large boats) carry heavy loads of grain, coal, and other products to places around the world. The state also has many other smaller rivers, with names like the Big Sioux, Turkey, and Skunk. They also helped carry early settlers and farm products around the state.

S is for state fair.

The Iowa State Fair is the biggest event held in Iowa. It is also one of the largest farm and industry shows in the country. About one million people visit it in Des Moines each August. They watch livestock contests, cheer at talent shows, see interesting displays like a cow carved from butter, and eat corn dogs. The first state fair was held in Fairfield in 1854. Much later, Phil Stong wrote a book, *State Fair*, based on his visits to the fair. The story was turned into a Broadway musical and several movies.

T is for tornadoes.

Only five states have more tornadoes than Iowa. These storms, with whirling winds and funnel clouds, usually happen in the spring and summer. They often appear with thunderstorms and can have the strongest winds on earth. The state's most deadly tornado happened in June 1860. Ninety-two people died and 175 were injured when the storm touched down near Clinton. About 1,500 tornadoes have been recorded in Iowa since 1950.

U is for universities.

Iowa has many very good universities and colleges. One of them is Iowa State University. It was created soon after President Abraham Lincoln helped make laws so that colleges were affordable for everyone. One of the state's oldest buildings is the Old Capitol in Iowa City, on the campus of the University of Iowa. The University of Northern Iowa is well known for its unusual covered stadium, called the UNI–Dome. Football games and other large events usually held outdoors take place there.

Vail Van Horne Van Meter Van Wert Ventura Victor Villisca Vincent Vinton Volga Vail

Van Horne Van Meter

THE BIRTHPLACE OF HERBERT HOOVER

SULLIVAN

V is for very important Iowans.

- Fran Allison, hostess of Kukla, Fran and Ollie, popular children's television show of the 1950s, was born in La Porte City in 1903.
- Carrie Chapman Catt, who fought for women's rights, grew up on a farm near Charles City in the 1870s.
- "Buffalo Bill" Cody, cowboy, buffalo hunter, and Wild West showman, was born in Scott County in 1846.
- Herbert Hoover, 31st president of the United States, was born in West Branch in 1874.
- John Wayne, popular Hollywood movie star, was born in Winterset in 1907.
- The five Sullivan brothers, who died together on the same ship in World War II, were born in Waterloo between 1914 and 1922.
- Laura Ingalls Wilder, author of the Little House books for young people, briefly lived in Burr Oak in the 1870s.

W is for Grant Wood.

Grant Wood, one of America's most famous artists, was born in Anamosa in 1891. His painting of a farmer and his daughter, called *American Gothic*, is one of the most popular paintings in the world. Many of his scenes are of the rolling hills and open spaces that he saw in eastern Iowa. He loved the area and spent most of his life there. He started the Stone City Art Colony and taught at the University of Iowa. Of all the many awards he received over the years for his art, he was proudest of the ribbons he won at the Iowa State Fair.

X is for oxen.

From 1830 to 1870, more than a million settlers moved into Iowa. Most of their wagons were pulled by oxen, animals that were stronger and cheaper to raise than horses. Oxen could eat sage and prairie grasses, which horses could not. These powerful animals were also used for farm work. Later on, they were replaced by tractors and other modern machines. You can still see oxen at work at Living History Farms near Des Moines.

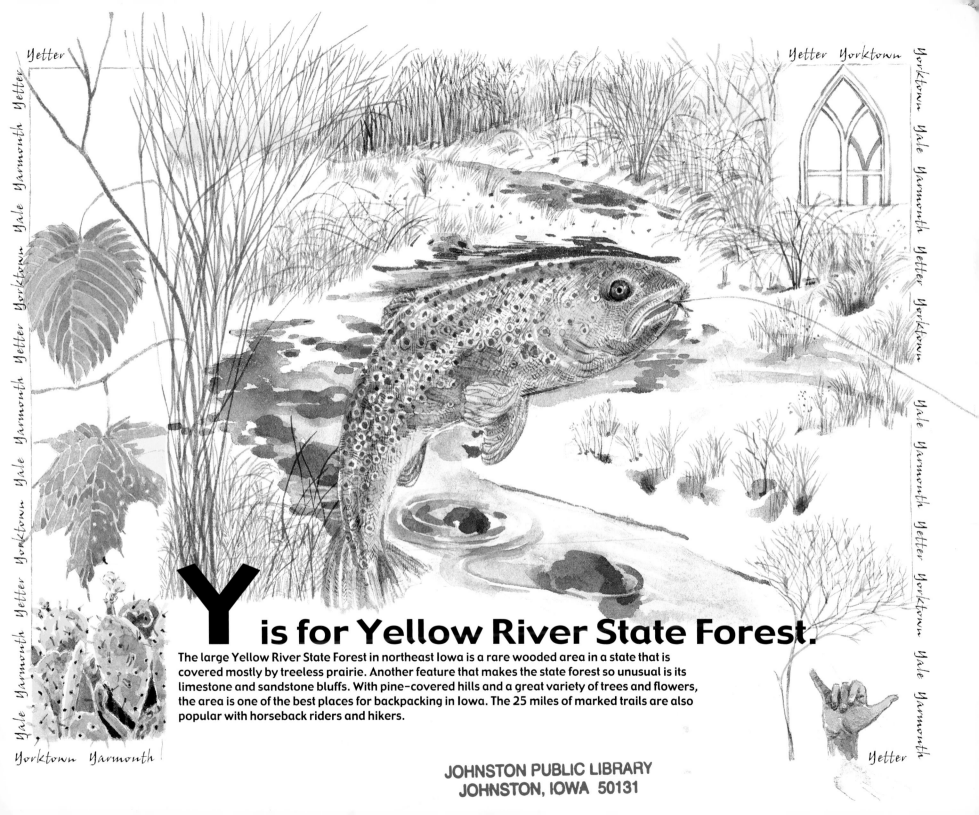

Y is for Yellow River State Forest.

The large Yellow River State Forest in northeast Iowa is a rare wooded area in a state that is covered mostly by treeless prairie. Another feature that makes the state forest so unusual is its limestone and sandstone bluffs. With pine–covered hills and a great variety of trees and flowers, the area is one of the best places for backpacking in Iowa. The 25 miles of marked trails are also popular with horseback riders and hikers.

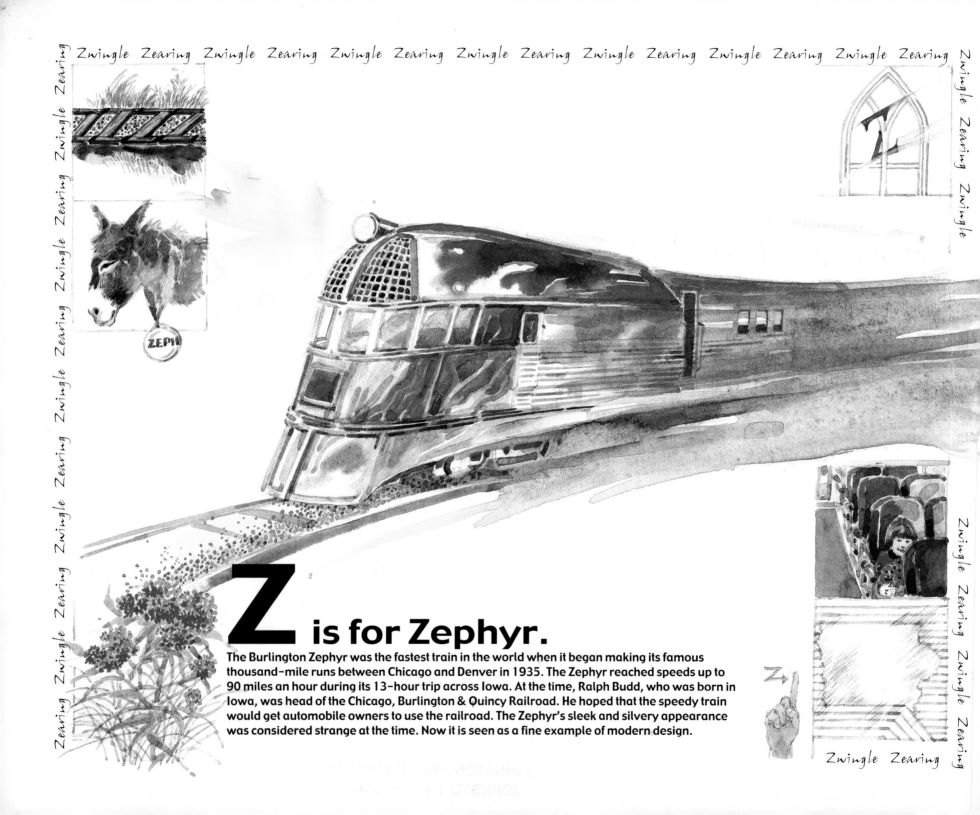

Z is for Zephyr.

The Burlington Zephyr was the fastest train in the world when it began making its famous thousand-mile runs between Chicago and Denver in 1935. The Zephyr reached speeds up to 90 miles an hour during its 13-hour trip across Iowa. At the time, Ralph Budd, who was born in Iowa, was head of the Chicago, Burlington & Quincy Railroad. He hoped that the speedy train would get automobile owners to use the railroad. The Zephyr's sleek and silvery appearance was considered strange at the time. Now it is seen as a fine example of modern design.

With Gratitude

The illustrator wishes to thank the following people for their help and for allowing the use of their photos as reference for three of the illustrations.

• Lee Maxwell, for Newton and the Maytag washing machines.

• Joan Liffring-Zug, *The Amanas Yesterday* and *The Amanas, A Photographic Journey, 1959-1999.*

• Kathie Lewis, Marketing Director of the Iowa State Fair and all the photographers and webmasters who put together the wonderful slide show and web page about the fair - www.iowastatefair.org.

MORE GREAT TITLES FROM TRAILS BOOKS & PRAIRIE OAK PRESS

KIDS BOOKS

ABCs Naturally, *Jay Wagner, Illustrated by Eileen Potts Dawson*

ABCs of Wisconsin , *Dori Hillestad Butler, Illustrated by Alison Relyea*

H is for Hawkeye, *Jay Wagner, Illustrated by Eileen Potts Dawson*

H is for Hoosier, *Dori Hillestad Butler, Illustrated by Eileen Potts Dawson*

W is for Wisconsin, *Dori Hillestad Butler, Illustrated by Eileen Potts Dawson*

Wisconsin Portraits: 55 People Who Made a Difference, *Martin Hintz*

Wisconsin Sports Heroes: 54 Athletes from A to Z, *Martin Hintz*

Travel Guides

Great Iowa Weekend Adventures, *Mike Whye*

Great Little Museums of the Midwest, *Christine des Garennes*

Great Minnesota Weekend Adventures, *Beth Gauper*

Minnesota Family Weekends, *Martin Hintz*

Minnesota Underground & the Best of the Black Hills, *Doris Green*

Tastes of Minnesota: A Food Lover's Tour, *Donna Tabbert Long*

Wisconsin Family Weekends: 20 Fun Trips for You and the Kids, *Susan Lampert Smith*

County Parks of Wisconsin, Revised Edition, *Jeannette and Chet Bell*

Up North Wisconsin: A Region for All Seasons, *Sharyn Alden*

Great Weekend Adventures, the *Editors of Wisconsin Trails*

Ghost Stories

Haunted Wisconsin, *Michael Norman and Beth Scott*

W-Files: True Reports of Wisconsin's Unexplained Phenomena, *Jay Rath*

M-Files: True Reports of Minnesota's Unexplained Phenomena, *Jay Rath*

I-Files: True Reports of Unexplained Phenomena in Illinois, *Jay Rath*

Northern Frights: A Supernatural Ecology of the Wisconsin Headwaters, *Dennis Boyer*

Giants in the Land: Folktales and Legends of Wisconsin, *Dennis Boyer*

For a free catalog, phone, write, or e-mail us.

Trails Books
P.O. Box 317, Black Earth, WI 53515
(800) 236-8088 • e-mail: books@wistrails.com
www.trailsbooks.com